Nasreddin Hoja Stories

**Stories are Selected and Translated from Turkish to English
by** *Evren Sener*

Edited By *Charise Diamond*

Copyright © 2013 Evren Sener

All rights reserved.

ISBN: 1492810517
ISBN-13: 978-1492810513

DEDICATION

To the Beloved.

CONTENTS

Life 8
Stories 12
    Why did Nasreddin Hoja Sit Backwards on the Donkey? 14
    If That One Talks This One Thinks 15
    The Caldron that Gave Birth! 16
    Nasreddin Hoja and the Beggar 17
    Novice Nightingale 18
    Hoja and the Hawk 19
    Hoja and the Thief 20
    The Turban of Hoja 21
    Where Do You Post the Letter? 22
    Hoja Visits the Mill 23
    Hoja Plays an Instrument 24
    The Greyhound 25
    Hoja Leavens the Lake 26
    The Steam of the Soup 27
    Money and the Whistle 28
    Hoja and His Mother-in-Law 29
    Hoja and His Donkey 30
    Letter and the Turban 31
    Hoja and His Neighbor 32
    On the Way Back Home 33
    Walnut and Pumpkin 34
    Hoja and His Son 35
    Where is the Cat? 36
    Hoja and His New House 37

The Worth of Gold	38
The End of the Sea	39
The Value of the Fur Coat	40
The House	41
Everyone is Right	43
Quince and Figs	44
The Donkey About to Get Used to	45
Living without Food	45
Lending Money	46
The Exchange	47
Hoja and the Thieves	48
The Man of His Word	49
Cash	50
The Flour on the Rope	51
It's My Accounting	52
Witness	53
The Judgment Day	54
Ninety-nine	55
Heat of the Star	56
To Fall from the Roof	58
Price of the King	59
Hoja as Sales Man	60
Dark at Night	61
Hoja's Donkey Got Lost	62
Sound of the Coat	63
Cabbage Soup	64

Maybe Me!	65
The Donkey	66
Why Does It Concern Me?	67
Extending Tongs	68
Smell of a Dream	69
I'm a Stranger in Here	70
The Ox	71
Bring My Coat	72
I Would Like to Die As Well	73
Hoja Goes Shopping	74
Something Valuable	75
Job Description	76
The Cure for Insomnia	77
The Feed of the Donkey	78
King's Dream	79
King's Elephant	80
The Cat and the Axe	81
Beaten by a Stick	82
Nothing	83
To Be Saved from Death	84
Lost	85
Thieves and the Donkey	86
Go Further	87
What Is There to Be Afraid of?	88
The Candle Light	89
Visits a Lot	90

Angel of Death 91

If She Was Not Dead 92

Spring 93

Thief and the Prayer 94

Weak Old Horse 95

Bow Down in Front of the Lord 97

The Donkey Can Read 98

Blessing of God 99

Which One is My Foot? 100

The Quilt 101

The Yogurt and the Vinegar 102

The Blind Fight 103

The Taste of the Grape 104

Share by God or by Hoja 105

Take My Hand 106

The Punishment of the Fox 107

Grape 108

I Know What To Do! 109

The Wife's Nagging 110

You Could Not Be Half of Your Son! 111

Three Scholars 112

Hunting Water Buffalo with a Crow 114

Between the Man and the God 116

Sources 120

Appendix 124

    Footnotes 126

Life

The great Turkish mystic, **Nasreddin Hoja**, is known for his many funny story/jokes which teach sincerity, patience, tolerance and persistence. His jokes are never rude or ugly and hurt no one. He tries to light the world with his advice and teachings. His repartee is sharp but naïve at the same time; giving his teachings a unique flavor. Never the pessimist, always the optimist, he has a cheerful nature and is a typical, affectionate father-figure of Anatolia. With his wisdom hidden in story/jokes, he shows how to get over/under/around the challenges in life and points out the path to those who are lost and in trouble. His enlightened humor causes people to think while laughing their way to the Truth.

Nasreddin Hoja was the contemporary of Rumi. They even lived in the same region in Turkey. He was born in the village of Sivrihisar in Turkey. His actual birth date is not known. It is known that after he studied in a madrasa[1] in Sivrihisar, he moved to Aksehir, another city in Turkey, in 1237 and lived there till the end of his life. He lived his life as a scholar, sometimes as a judge and sometimes as an imam[2]. His wife, his son, kids of the neighbors, artisans, mullahs, villagers, thieves and his donkey are the main characters in his story/jokes.

These are translations of some famous jokes of Nasreddin Hoja which are part of the Turkish national culture. They became known by being told from generation to generation. The Nasreddin Hoja Joke Books are just a collection of known stories so there are no volumes of books as well. There is no written manuscript by Nasreddin Hoja himself or anyone else. People around him passed his stories along, continuing until present time and made him live for centuries. He is still known, respected and loved in Turkey as if he were still alive.

Stories

Why did Nasreddin Hoja Sit Backwards on the Donkey?

One day Hoja was going to class with his students. He sat facing the rear of the donkey. They all wondered why he was facing backwards on the donkey and asked him the reason. "Hoja, why did you sit backwards?"

He replied: "If I sit in the regular position you'll be facing my back and if I let you walk in front of me then I will be facing your back. In this way, however, we face each other. It is better to walk face to face."

If That One Talks This One Thinks

One day Hoja was walking in the market place and saw a parrot on sale for a high price. Seeing this he told himself, "So, nowadays a bird makes good money."

The next day, taking his turkey with him, he ran to the market place and started yelling: "This turkey is for sale for twelve gold coins!"

Hearing this, the people were amused and approached him saying, "Oh, Hoja! Isn't it too much to ask twelve gold coins for an ordinary turkey like that?"

Hoja replied: "Why not? Yesterday, a tiny bird was on sale for ten gold coins. This is a huge turkey which deserves more."

The people replied: "But Hoja that was no ordinary bird. It was a parrot. "

Hoja said, "We understand that it was a parrot but in the end it was a bird. What is its specialty?"

The people replied, "Of course it had an outstanding specialty. That bird has the ability to speak and it speaks very well."

Hoja, pointing to the turkey he was holding under his arm said, "If that bird speaks this one thinks- and it thinks very well."

The Caldron that Gave Birth!

One day Hoja borrowed his neighbor's caldron. When he gave it back he placed a small stewpot inside. Seeing the stewpot, his neighbor asked, "What is that?"

Hoja replied, "Congratulations! Your caldron gave birth."

Hearing this, his neighbor got very happy. After a couple of days Hoja visited his neighbor to borrow the caldron again. The man gladly loaned it.

Quite some time passed after that day but Hoja did not bring the caldron back. Noticing this, the man visited Hoja to ask for his caldron back. He curiously asked, "What happened to my caldron? You took it but did not bring it back."

Hoja replied in sorrow, "Accept my condolences! I am sorry but your caldron is dead."

The man asked in bewilderment, "Oh Hoja how is it possible? Can a caldron ever die?"

Hoja replied in the same relaxed manner, "My dear neighbor you're talking nonsense! You previously believed that the caldron gave birth so why don't you believe that it has died? Why should a caldron not die if it can give birth?"

Nasreddin Hoja and the Beggar

One day Hoja climbed on the roof of his house. His intention was to fix it before winter arrived. The moment he started working, the doorbell rang. He looked down to see the visitor. There was a stranger waiting at the door. Seeing him, Hoja asked, "What do you want?"

The stranger said, "Dear Hoja, can you please come downstairs? I have something to tell you."

Hoja became curious so, dragging his heavy old body, he went downstairs, passing through all the floors and stairs. When he reached the entrance he was breathless. Ashe opened the door the man started begging by showing his empty hands. "Please give me some alms for the sake of the Lord."

Hearing this Hoja did not respond but he signaled to the man to follow him upstairs. He was in the front and the man was behind him as they both climbed up the high stairs. They were both breathless when they reached the roof. Turning to the man and pointing upward, Hoja said, "Ask for alms from the Lord, I have nothing to give."

Novice Nightingale

Passing by a fruit orchard, Hoja was attracted to the trees full of all types of fruit. Not calculating the consequences, he climbed an apricot tree. Plucking the apricots he started eating one after another.

Suddenly he heard somebody yelling at him, asking what he was doing up in the apricot tree. Looking down, Hoja saw the gardener waiting for an answer and holding a stick in his hand.

Bending towards the man, Hoja spoke timidly. "I am a nightingale. While I was flying by I landed in this tree."

Hearing this, the gardener spoke; "Beautiful and enchanting is the song of the nightingale. Please sing to me so I will enjoy your sound."

To be able to escape from the gardener, Hoja started singing with his terrible out-of-tune sound. Not knowing where to run and hide to be able to avoid that sound, the gardener yelled at Hoja in panic, "Enough! What is this? Do you think that I have never ever heard the sound of the nightingale?"

In an ashamed, humble voice Hoja said, "Don't expect to hear the sound that you are used to. The novice nightingale sings only that well!"

Hoja and the Hawk

As Hoja was chatting with his friends, they started talking about some cooking recipes. They praised one certain dish so much that Hoja decided to cook it as well, so he took notes.

After leaving his friends he ran to the market and bought the required ingredients. He walked out of the market holding his package with one hand and holding the recipe with the other hand.

On his way back home, suddenly a hawk appeared, swiped the package from his hand and flew away. He chased the bird for a while but he could not catch it. Finally he let it go. Waving the recipe in his hand he yelled at the bird, "You took the ingredients but you left the recipe on how to cook it. You can never cook and enjoy it."

Hoja and the Thief

One night a thief broke into Hoja's stable and stole his donkey. In the morning when he noticed the absence of his donkey he started yelling. Hearing his cries, the neighbors gathered together at his front door.

As soon as they learned what had happened, everybody started giving his opinion. "Maybe you forgot to lock the door," said one of the neighbors.

"Look at this! How can you call it a door?" said the other.

"Why can't you hear anything? How is it possible not to hear such a noise?" said another neighbor.

Listening to these remarks, Hoja realized that instead of consoling him they were putting the blame on him. Finally he interrupted, "Please have some mercy! So you all think that I'm guilty. How about the thief? Isn't he guilty at all?"

The Turban of Hoja

Whenever Hoja saw the children playing, he could not help watching them. He enjoyed and loved watching them running and jumping around.

One day, while he was watching them, a kid grabbed Hoja's turban and ran away. Even though he tried to catch the boy, he could not succeed. The children started tossing it to one another. Even though he told them, "Don't do it," none of them listened.

Watching his turban being passed from hand to hand, Hoja gave up struggling and headed back to his home.

Seeing him without his turban, his wife asked curiously, "What happened? Where is your turban?"

Hoja replied, "My turban remembered its childhood so it started playing with the children in the neighborhood."

Where Do You Post the Letter?

An illiterate came to visit Hoja to get him to write a letter. The illiterate said, "You know how to write. Can you please write down what I say?"

Before he took the pen and paper Hoja asked, "Where are you going to send this letter?"

"Bagdad," the illiterate answered.

"I cannot go there." Hoja replied.

Thinking that Hoja misunderstood him he said, "No Hoja, the letter will go, not you."

Hoja answered, "That's true but to be able to read it, I should also go there."

Hoja Visits the Mill

Since there was no flour left at home, Hoja visited the mill. He had his bag full of wheat. Being an honest man, the miller worked without respect to personal relationships of any kind. He put all his clients in order, grinding their wheat according to their arrival time. Having no other choice, Hoja put his bag into the cue and started waiting.

After waiting for a while he got tired and was tempted to speed things up in his favor. He started taking the flour from the other bags and filling his own bag. When the miller saw what he was doing he felt offended and also thought this behavior was not appropriate for Hoja so he interfered, saying: "Oh Hoja, what are you doing?"

Being busted, Hoja was stunned but came back to himself and quickly answered, "Sorry, such a fool I am! Do I know what am I doing?"

Being an honest man, the miller did not believe what he said and questioned Hoja further, saying, "What I have been able to observe so far is that you take the flour from the other bags and put it into yours. Does a fool act in such a way? Why don't you put flour into the other empty bags instead of yours?"

Without paying attention to the miller, Hoja replied, "Indeed I am a fool but not such a fool as that."

Hoja Plays an Instrument

At a dinner party, the guests asked Hoja whether he knew how to play a particular stringed instrument. Hoja said, "Yes."

Hearing this, they brought the instrument and gave it to him to play. They said, "So now play and let us enjoy your music."

Taking the instrument, he started playing. A terrible sound started arising. His fingers did not move and he held them at the same spot, continuing to hit the same cord. In a panic, they tried to stop him. They interfered and asked, "Oh Hoja! How can you play this instrument in such a way? We noticed that your fingers are fixed in the same spot and do not move at all."

Hearing this Hoja smiled. "Do not bother! The other players who played this instrument before me were also looking for this spot. Since I have found it, I do not have to move my fingers."

The Greyhound

A miserly merchant asked Hoja to help him find a greyhound. He said, "If you bring me a proper dog I will also make you happy. I want a dog with long ears like a rabbit, a waist like an ant and legs like a gazelle. I want a slender greyhound in such a shape and form as I described."

After a couple of days Hoja visited him with an ordinary bulky shepherd dog and it was exactly the opposite of the dog that the merchant had described. The miserly merchant first looked at the dog then at Hoja and in bewilderment he spoke: "Oh Hoja, are you mocking me? How is anyone supposed to go hunting with such a beast? I asked for a slender dog for hunting and you brought this!"

Hearing this Hoja replied, "Have no worries. Let it stay with a stingy merchant like you for some time. It will definitely lose weight and turn out to be a slender greyhound."

Hoja Leavens the Lake

Hoja took a bowl of yogurt and walked to the big lake of the town. Seeing him going to the lake people thought that he was going to enjoy eating yogurt near the lake. Hoja, however, was a man of surprises so they could not help wondering what he might do near the lake and they followed him. When they arrived at the lake, they saw that Hoja was sitting there pouring yogurt, spoon by spoon, into the lake instead of eating it.

They got closer to him and asked, "Oh, Hoja! What are you doing?"

Hoja replied, "Don't you understand? By adding yogurt I am leavening the lake. In this way I will turn it into yogurt."

Upon hearing this, the people started laughing. "Oh Hoja! Can a lake ever be turned into yogurt?"

Smiling Hoja nodded his head, "I know that as well, but just imagine what would happen if it actually turned into yogurt."

The Steam of the Soup

While Hoja was working as a judge, a cook sued a poor man. He said, "This man held his bread in the steam of the soup and then ate it. The price, whatever I have asked, should be paid to me. Even when I claimed he owed me and insisted, he refused to pay."

Hoja asked the poor fellow whether he wanted to say or add something to the story of the cook.

The poor man replied, "What can I pay? It is true that I held my bread in the steam of his soup but I did not eat one bite of the soup."

After listening to them both, Hoja gave his decision and called the cook aside. Taking his small coin bag out of his pocket he shook it near the cook's ear. "Hear the sound of the coins and take it as your payment. If you only sold the steam of the food you only get the sound of the coins as payment. Now, since you have gotten your payment, you may leave the court. Your case is closed."

Money and the Whistle

Whenever Hoja went to the market the children of the neighborhood crowded around him and begged him to buy something for them. Every time they requested something, Hoja used to buy it for them. On one of these days the children asked him to buy whistles but only one of them gave him money. After accepting their request, Hoja continued on his way to market.

When his shopping was finished, he started on his way back home. The children saw him coming, intercepted him and asked for their whistles. Upon hearing this request, Hoja took only one whistle out of his pocket and gave it to the boy who had paid for it. When the children saw this, they objected and asked why.

Hoja replied, "Do not take offense. The one who pays plays the whistle."

Hoja and His Mother-in-Law

When Hoja's mother-in-law was washing clothes by the wild river she fell in the water. They informed Hoja, called on him for help and all started looking for her together. Hoja started walking by the river in case she might have succeeded in holding on to a branch or a rock, hoping to find her alive.

After a while the crowd noticed that Hoja was walking in the opposite direction of the flow of the stream. In bewilderment they yelled at him, "Oh Hoja why are you walking in the opposite direction of the stream? If you want to find her you should be looking for her in the same direction not the opposite. Is it possible that she was dragged in the opposite direction of the stream?"

Hoja, nodding his head, said, "You don't know what type of a person she is. She is so dour that she opposes everything. Do you think that she would go with the flow when she falls into the river?"

Hoja and His Donkey

Upon deciding to sell his donkey, Hoja took it to the marketplace and turned it over to the animal merchant. To find customers, the merchant started loudly and cheerfully praising the animal. However, the donkey kicked everyone who tried to approach and bit everyone who tried to touch it. Long story short, the donkey kept everyone away who tried to come close. Trying to load weight on it or hold it from the bridle was not an option.

Being fed up with the donkey's actions, clients complained so the merchant spoke to Hoja, "Oh Hoja! It is not possible to find a client for such a donkey. Please take it back to your home."

Hoja, holding the donkey from its bridle, said, "To tell the truth, my intention was not to sell it. I brought it to the market place to show everyone what I am going through every day with this animal and how much I am suffering."

Letter and the Turban

A man visited Hoja. He brought a letter for him to read. He said "I received a letter but I couldn't read it. Can you please read it for me?"

Taking the letter in hand, Hoja tried to read it but he couldn't because it was written in Arabic. Making a small, embarrassed sound he sadly said, "Sorry I cannot help you because I cannot read it."

When the man heard this he got frustrated. Instead of thanking Hoja and looking for someone else to read the letter he started insulting him. "You cannot even read a letter and you call yourself Hoja[3], a scholar? Shame on you! Curse your title as scholar. Shame on your huge turban that you wear so high on your head, showing what a high-class scholar you are!"

After the man's strong reaction, Hoja could not hold himself back any longer. Taking his turban off his head, he placed it on the other man's head. "If the trick is in the turban, now that you are wearing it you can read the letter."

Hoja and His Neighbor

Hoja had a neighbor who, from time to time, asked to borrow his donkey. To be polite, Hoja used to lend his donkey. However, the man started requesting it so often that Hoja decided to end this situation.

One day the man requested his donkey again. Hoja said: "It is absent. It took the wheat to the mill."

Suddenly, but just as a coincidence, the donkey started hee-hawing. Upon hearing this, the man laughed and said, "Oh Hoja! You say that it is absent but what is this sound? Isn't it your donkey hee-hawing?"

Hoja replied in the same firm manner, "Shame on you! You with this long white beard of wisdom; you don't believe my word as Hoja but you believe the donkey?"

On the Way Back Home

On his way back home something unexpected and unfortunate happened to Hoja. In front of the kids playing in the street, Hoja's donkey lost its balance and Hoja fell to the ground. When the children saw him fall down they started laughing and mocking him.

As was his nature, however, Hoja did not bother at all. He acted as if nothing had happened and he did not understand why they were laughing. In bewilderment he spoke, "You naughty kids! Why do you laugh so much? I was going to get off my donkey when I arrived home."

Walnut and Pumpkin

Hoja had a small garden and he did gardening whenever he found time. On one such day, feeling tired, he sat down under a walnut tree and started looking over his garden.

Suddenly the pumpkins grabbed his attention. The plant had a slender, tiny vine bearing a huge harvest. Then he turned his head towards the walnuts hanging in the tree over his head. The tree had a thick, heavy trunk but its product was small and tiny.

Seeing this difference he was amazed and couldn't solve this dilemma. He said, "Oh God! How did you decide to grow these tiny walnuts on the tree instead of these huge pumpkins? Wouldn't it be more proper to grow pumpkins in this tree? "

At that moment a walnut fell off the tree and crashed on the top of his head. Feeling this he raised his arms towards the sky and spoke, "Oh God! From now on I will never ever question or criticize you. What would have happened to me if this huge pumpkin had grown in the tree and fell on me?"

Hoja and His Son

One day Hoja called his son and when he arrived he slapped his face. Then he gave the water jug to his son and spoke: "Take this and go to the fountain. After filling it with water bring it back and don't break it."

Seeing this, one of his neighbors asked furiously, "Oh Hoja! What have you done? Can a child be beaten *before* he breaks the water jug?"

Hoja smiled and explained, "If you are going to beat him, beat him before he breaks the jug. What is the use of beating him after he breaks the jug?"

Where is the Cat?

One day Hoja went grocery shopping and brought home 2 pounds of ingredients. After telling his wife to cook a nice dish for dinner he left. His wife, however, cooked the food and then feasted with her friends. When Hoja arrived for dinner she served plain rice and some bread.

Looking at what he had been served, he asked, "What has happened to the groceries I bought? Where is the food? I told you to cook something nice for tonight."

Hoja's wife responded, "Oh! You don't know what has happened! I cooked a very nice meal but the cat ate it all."

Hoja got furious when he heard this. "What?!! Has it eaten all the food?? Thief!" Jumping up in anger, he got his wooden stick and started searching for the cat.

Suddenly the cat showed up but it seemed so skinny, just as it always was. Seeing its condition, Hoja got suspicious. He thought to himself, "How could it be that skinny after eating such a full meal?"

He brought the weighing scale and weighed the cat. The cat weighed 2 pounds. Now he questioned his wife. "The cat weighs 2 pounds. The groceries I bought also weighed 2pounds. If the cat ate them all where is the weight of the groceries? If this weight is the groceries where is the cat?"

Hoja and His New House

A rumor was heard in the neighborhood that Hoja had moved into a new house. Out of curiosity, people decided to visit him. When they arrived at the location, they saw him sitting in front of a wall that was standing in a garden. Other than that, there was no such thing as a house.

Approaching him they asked curiously, "Oh Hoja, what are you doing here?"

He pleasantly smiled and replied, "Oh, welcome! I am sitting in the garden of my new house."

The bewildered crowd asked curiously, "Oh Hoja! This is only one wall. Where is the house?"

Hoja replied confidently, "You see that I have one wall. The only thing I need is a roof, 3 other walls and a door. Why shouldn't I call this as a house?" [4]

The Worth of Gold

One day, while Hoja was in town, a man came up to him. Holding a piece of gold in his hand he asked Hoja a favor, "Can you turn this gold into cash?"

Poor Hoja did not have any money in his pocket. He intended to get rid of the man. "I am busy now. Come back in two hours."

But the man insisted, "Unfortunately I am in a hurry. Please do help me."

Having no way out, Hoja reluctantly agreed to help the man. Taking the gold in his hand he looked around helplessly. "This gold is worthless. I cannot turn it into cash."

The man insisted, however, so Hoja said, "This gold is below its worth by more than a few coins."

"I accept whatever you give for it," the man said.

Now the situation had become weirder. Hoja did not want anyone to learn that he was penniless.

"You see the gold. What will you give for it?" the man asked once again.

"The gold is much below its worth. If you measure you too will discover this. If you listen to me you won't turn it into cash. If you insist that I turn it into cash, you should give the gold plus 6 coins to me."

The End of the Sea

One day Hoja got on board a boat. He sat near the rudder. After watching the sailor for a while and noticing how he steered the rudder he thought that it was an easy job to do.

Coming closer to the sailor he asked, "Dear brother, you may not know me but you can leave your task to me. You can sit aside, rest and sleep. Have confidence in me that I can easily use that rudder."

Believing in Hoja's words, the naïve sailor left the rudder to him and sat off to the side. For some time Hoja sailed without any problem. When they approached land, however, a big wave came from the side and hit the boat hard.

Consequently the boat became stranded. Scared passengers started yelling in panic, "What is going on? Oh, Hoja, what have you done?"

Not taking offense, Hoja calmly responded, "I did not do anything. The sea just ended!"

The Value of the Fur Coat

One day Hoja was invited to a dining party in a rich man's house. He went there wearing his casual clothes. Since Hoja was not a rich man, his clothes were old and full of patches and mended seams. Seeing his clothes and poor appearance, the guests did not pay attention to him. Nobody greeted him or spoke to him. After being seated at the dining table, their behaviors continued. Nobody even served food to him.

Noticing these unpleasant behaviors, Hoja got frustrated and he suddenly got up from the table and ran back to his house. Walking straight to his bedroom closet he took out a fur coat. After putting it on, he immediately went back to the dining party.

The behavior of the guests changed suddenly when they saw him wearing a fur coat. People greeted him and they tried to speak to him one after the other. Then he sat back down at the dining table and they served soup in his bowl.

Suddenly Hoja took one edge of his fur coat and dipped it into the soup. "Oh Hoja, what are you doing?" the bewildered people asked when they saw him do this.

He answered, "When I first sat at this table nobody spoke to me and no one served food to me as if I was invisible. After wearing this coat everything has changed and I have suddenly become visible. Since I gained recognition with this garment, it deserves to drink the soup. Eat, my fur coat, eat!"

The House

One day a man came to visit Hoja. He started complaining and crying about the size of his house. He said he was living there with his wife and their child. Since he was poor he could not afford to move into a bigger house so he felt sad that he was stuck there.

After listening to the man, Hoja asked, "Do you have cows?"

The man replied, "Yes, I have two cows."

Hoja said, "Go back to your house and take them in. Do not ask any more questions."

Because of his respect for Hoja, the man silently went back to his house and did as Hoja ordered.

He came back after 3 days and said, "Oh Hoja, after taking the cows in the house looks even smaller. Please find a solution."

Ignoring what he said, Hoja asked, "Do you have goats?"

The man said, "Yes I have 5 goats."

Hoja said, "Now go back to your house and take those 5 goats also in the house and do not ask any further questions."

Because of his respect, the man asked no more questions and went back to his house and took the 5 goats into his house. Now the house was more crowded than ever. There was less space than ever before.

After 3 days he ran back to Hoja. "Oh Hoja! Now the house is smaller than before. There is not much space for me, my wife and our child. Please help us!"

Hoja once again acted as if he did not hear what the poor fellow said and he asked, "Are your parents alive?"

The man replied, "Yes they are."

Hoja said, "Do you have other animals?"

The man replied, "Yes I have 6 chickens and a dog."

Hoja said, "Now go back to your house and invite your parents to your house. Take your chickens and your dog into your house. Stay with them and do not visit me for 2 weeks."

With all his respect the man did not reject Hoja's wish. He did as Hoja said. First he took his chickens and dog into the house and then invited his parents. They all lived together for two weeks.

After two weeks he rushed into Hoja's house and begged Hoja to save him from the crowd. He said, "Oh Hoja, please help me. These past two weeks were like a hell. There is no space left in the house even to breathe. Please do not suggest that I take anyone or anything else into the house."

Hearing this Hoja smiled. "Now go back to your house, take all your animals out, and send your parents back home."

With Hoja's advice the man happily ran back to his house and did as Hoja suggested. The next day he came back to Hoja's house and spoke; "Dear Hoja, as you've said, I took all my animals out and sent my parents back home. After all had left, I realized that my house is indeed very big and there is lots of space."

Everyone is Right

One day 2 men looking for justice came to visit Hoja. Each was complaining about the other.
After listening to the first man's story, Hoja said, "You are right."

Suddenly the other one interrupted and told the story from his point of view. After listening to him Hoja said, "You are right too."

Meanwhile Hoja's wife was present in the room. After listening to Hoja's judgment, she interfered by saying, "Oh Hoja! How is it possible that both of them are right?"

"My wife," said Hoja, "you are also right!"

Quince and Figs

One day Hoja decided to present a fruit basket as a gift to the king. Thinking for a while which one to choose he decided to fill the basket with quinces[5]. Then he changed his mind and decided to take figs instead of quinces with him so he filled his basket with figs.

When he arrived at the palace, he presented the basket to the king[6]. Things went wrong however. Seeing his gift, the King got furious and took it as an insult. He started throwing figs at Hoja. However Hoja did not mind at all.

Seeing Hoja neither offended nor angry, but indeed very happy, the King got curious and asked, "Why are you happily smiling and thanking God?"

Hoja replied, "I am a lucky man. This basket was originally full of quinces. What would have happened to me if I had not replaced them with figs?"

The Donkey About to Get Used to Living without Food

Hoja was fed up with feeding his donkey. It was not satiated easily. The donkey ate as much as it was fed and never felt full.

Seeing his donkey eating as much as he put in front of it, Hoja decided to try a trick. He started to feed it less and less every day and the donkey did not react. It seemed to be satisfied with its daily amount of food.

One day when Hoja came to the stable, he saw the dead body of the poor animal. Seeing his donkey dead, Hoja felt sorry but he did not drop his sarcastic attitude and spoke into its ear, "You were about to get used to living without food."

Lending Money

One day Hoja's neighbor came to visit him. Explaining his problems in business he asked to borrow some money. He offered to repay the loan but not right away, only over a long period of time.

Not pleased with this offer, Hoja spoke, "So you ask to return my money in time? I will handle your request with care. I will help you but you should also help me. Do not ask for *both* the money and paying in time from me. I'll give you the time but ask for the money from someone else."

The Exchange

One day, when Hoja was out walking, somebody slapped his neck. The sound of the slap echoed even in his brain. He furiously turned to face the man who had slapped his neck. He was surprised to see a stranger, someone that he had never seen before.

Having no shame the man spoke, "Oh Hoja! Sorry, I thought you were someone else."

Since Hoja was a clever man he did not believe this and took him directly to the court. He told what had happened and complained about the man. His neck was still hurting even while he was speaking. However the judge did not pay much attention to his story. Since the judge was the man's friend, he gave a punishment that was almost in favor of the man. He sentenced the man to pay two small coins.

Hoja got more frustrated and opposed the sentence. "Only two small coins in exchange for a slap? This is not even money!"

Since the man who slapped Hoja was a penniless idle, he asked the judge to give him some time to find the required amount. As the judge gladly accepted this offer, the man freely walked away.

The judge and Hoja started waiting for him to come back. The hours followed each other. The judge and Hoja waited for him to come back but the man did not show up. At the peak of his anger, Hoja approached the judge and slapped his neck. The judge was so bewildered by this act, he showed no reaction.

Hoja, ignoring the situation, calmly walked to the door. Before he went out, he said to the judge, "Now I am leaving. Goodbye to you! You can now wait for the coins in exchange for the slap!"

Hoja and the Thieves

In the middle of the night, thieves broke into Hoja's house. Neither his wife nor his son noticed them. However Hoja was alert and acted as if he was asleep.

The thieves picked up whatever they found such as a table and chairs and started carrying them out. The only things that they left were the beds and blankets covering the sleeping household. When they finished their work, the thieves sneaked out of Hoja's house.

After watching all this, Hoja picked up his blanket and walked behind the thieves. Wherever they went he followed them. Finally they stopped in front of a house. Taking out their keys, they walked into their own house. Hoja walked in right after them.

The thieves were bewildered when they saw him. "Oh Hoja! What are you doing in here?"

Hoja chuckled and acted as if he was bewildered. "Oh! Because you carried all the stuff from my house to here, I thought we moved to this house, didn't we?"

The Man of His Word

One day a stranger invited Hoja to his house "Come and visit me someday and let us eat salt and bread together."

Hearing this pleased Hoja. Dreaming of a rich and delicious dinner table, he visited the man as soon as possible.

During the dinner, as the man had formerly mentioned, only salt and bread were served. When he saw this, Hoja's dreams of a delicious meal collapsed. His hopes faded away and he even came to the brink of crying. He patiently accepted this whim of destiny however. First he thanked God then he ate what was served to him.

After they finished their bread a man knocked at the door. The poor fellow said, "I am very hungry. I have not eaten anything since morning. I'm begging for your help."

The householder got angry and said, "Ask God."

The poor fellow insisted. As the beggar continued to plead, the host got even angrier. "Go away! Otherwise I'll beat the hell out of you and crush your head."

Ignoring what the householder said, the poor fellow kept on begging. As Hoja was sitting there listening to all of this, he interfered in a panic. "Hey you!" he said "Look at me! It is better that you listen to him and go away! You do not know him but he does exactly what he says. He is a man of his word."

Cash

Sometime ago Hoja had borrowed some money from his neighbor. To request the money back, his neighbor visited Hoja every morning. He would say, "Hoja, isn't it enough? Please pay me back the amount you've borrowed."

Hoja responded frequently, "Believe me, I think about this payment day and night. Wouldn't I pay you if I had such an amount? Wouldn't I call you myself if I were able to pay? Wouldn't I visit you myself and make the payment? However, I do not have it. If God gives it to me I'll give it to you."

After this conversation his neighbor did not visit Hoja anymore. Days turned into weeks and weeks became months but Hoja was not able to pay his debt. One day, however, Hoja went to visit his neighbor. "I have good news for you. Soon you'll get your money back," he said.

His neighbor got very happy with this news and asked, "When?"

Hoja said, "Soon!"

The man insisted, "Soon when?"

Hoja replied, "I have planted the seeds of thorn bushes all along the road."

His neighbor looked him with blank eyes and asked, "So? Why did you plant thorns? I do not understand anything."

Hoja explained as follows: "This plant is a treasure. The thorns will soon start growing. As you know, lots of shepherds pass along this road. Their wool will be hooked on these thorns and I will collect it. Then I will make ropes and I will make sweaters and sell them in the market. In this way I will pay my debt to you."

Upon hearing this, his neighbor started laughing. Noticing him laughing, Hoja said, "Seeing the cash made you smile."

The Flour on the Rope

One day Hoja's neighbor visited him. He wanted to borrow Hoja's rope to hang laundry for drying. Hoja was reluctant to lend his rope so he started making up many excuses.

Finally he said, "I cannot give it to you because today I will spread flour on it."

After hearing this, his neighbor asked in amusement, "Oh Hoja! How can it be possible to hang flour on the rope? "

Hoja got angry. "If a person is not willing to lend his rope then it becomes possible to hang flour on the rope."

It's My Accounting

It had been rumored that the tax officer transferred a huge amount of money to his personal account instead of to the treasury. After noticing this, the king got mad and as punishment he made the tax officer eat all the documents on which he had registered all the untrue payments.

Taking all the tax officer's amulets, rights and duties back, the king gave them to Hoja and assigned him as his new tax officer. Resisting the king's command or rejecting this call of duty was not possible so Hoja unwillingly accepted this new task. The King left after ordering Hoja to come back with the new accounts in one month's time.

After a month when Hoja was summoned, he entered the King's chamber with loaves of bread. Seeing all these loaves of bread, the king got curious and asked, "What is all this nonsense about?"

Hoja replied, "I kept the accounts on the bread instead of paper; that's why I brought all these loaves here."

King asked, "Why? How can you keep the accounts on the bread loaves?"

Hoja answered calmly, "Sorry, but am I not the one who has to eat the accounts in case you find a mistake?"

Witness

Being an honest man, Hoja always spoke the truth and clearly told what he thought. One day a group of people visited to convince him to bear witness on their behalf at the court. From their point of view they were right but they had been treated unjustly at the court.

It was a simple case about wheat so Hoja agreed to witness on their behalf. They also proposed to pay 1000 coins to him in case they won.

They all went to the court together. Many questions were asked of other witnesses and their stories were listened to. The case was about to be concluded on the group's behalf.

Finally Hoja's testimony was also needed. Thus the judge asked him to tell the story. Hoja, however, started talking about barley instead of wheat. That grabbed the attention of the careful judge and he questioned Hoja's mistake. "Oh, Hoja, you are talking about barley instead of wheat? Why?"

Hoja smiled and replied, "Why should it matter whether I talk about wheat or barley when the whole story is merely a lie?"

The Judgment Day

A few of Hoja's neighbors came to visit him. Their intention was to have a free feast from Hoja. They said, "Hoja, there is a rumor that tomorrow or the next day the world will come to an end and it will be the judgment day. Thus it is nonsense to save your money or keep your food in storage. Give us a feast so we may happily and merrily enjoy our last moments."

Hoja did not react but accepted their offer. He took out the food he had saved and went to the field near the lake to prepare the feast.

First he started the fire for cooking and then chopped the vegetables. Meanwhile his neighbors arrived. Glad to see him cooking, they decided to enjoy the beautiful weather and after taking off their clothes they jumped into the lake to go swimming.

Hoja silently collected their clothes and threw them into the fire. Then he called them to come and dine with him. However, without their clothes the men could not come to dinner and asked him for their clothes.

Hoja spoke, "What nonsense to ask for your clothes at such a time when the world is about to come to an end and the Day of Judgment is today or tomorrow. I didn't think that you would need your clothes any longer so I threw them in the fire which helped me cook the food. Now eat, enjoy the food and be merry."

Ninety-nine

One night, in his dream, Hoja met Khidr[7] who told him that he would give him 100 gold coins. Hoja felt so happy when he heard this. Khidr started counting the gold coins one by one into Hoja's hand but he stopped counting at ninety-nine.

At this, Hoja got frustrated and complained, "You said that you'd give me 100 gold coins but you've stopped at 99. I definitely do not accept that amount. You either round it off to 100 or take it back."

In reply, Khidr said, "You fool." Ending with these words he vanished with the gold and the dream was over.

Hoja suddenly woke up in his poor house on his bed made of straw. Looking around at all of this he realized what a huge mistake he had made and that he had missed a great opportunity. Thus he tried to go back to his dream.

He said, "Oh dear Khidr, please forgive me! Condemn the one who insisted on 100! Give me back the coins no matter whether they are 100 or 99!"

Heat of the Star

The intention of Hoja's neighbors was to have a free dinner from Hoja. Thus they made a bet with him. They made an offer: "If you can stay all night long in the open field and stand the cold, we will give you a feast but if you cannot stand the cold and come back to your home earlier, you'll give us a feast.

Hoja gladly accepted their offer and went to the open field when the sun was setting. Unluckily, the weather was extremely cold but he tried his best and waited until dawn, dreaming about the amazing, delicious dishes that he would eat. When the sun was coming up over the horizon, he walked back to his house. He was so happy to win the bet.

His neighbors, however, had no intention of letting him win the bet and losing their chance of having a free meal. Thus they said to him, "You've lost the bet, you had to stay there until the morning in the cold without any heating."

Hoja replied, "I did stay outside in the field until dawn without any heating."

Rejecting his assertion, the men insisted on their claim. "Last night the sky was full of stars and you heated yourself by these stars."

In bewilderment and disbelief Hoja asked, "I heated myself with the stars?"

They insisted, "Yes, you've heated yourself with these stars. Thus you've lost the bet. Tonight we'll visit you for the feast. Don't make us wait too long and cook the food before the sun sets."

Realizing that there was no way out, Hoja accepted the situation. "Ok, so tonight come and have your feast."

When the sun was setting the neighbors came to his house one by one. Before they went to the dining room they sat for a while in the living room. All of them were dreaming of amazing food being cooked. However it seemed to be taking ages. They waited patiently but it was as if time was passing very slowly. After a couple of hours they were starving and finally they rebelled all together and asked when the food was going to be ready.

Hoja replied comfortably, "No need to hurry; it is being cooked."

Their patience was exhausted at this point, and they insisted on seeing the cooked food. Hoja gladly guided them through the kitchen and showed them the kettle over a burning candle.

"Oh Hoja," they asked in bewilderment, "What is this? How can you call this cooking? How can food be cooked with candle light?"

Hoja replied comfortably, "Dear fellow neighbors, no need to worry! Please comfort yourselves. If I was able to heat myself with the light of the stars, then this candle should not only cook but even burn the food."

To Fall from the Roof

One day Hoja climbed to the roof of his house to check if it needed to be repaired. While he was checking, due to a careless move, he fell to the ground. Because of immense pain, he started screaming and his neighbors ran to help. A crowd gathered around him and started asking him questions.

"Oh, Hoja, how did this happen? Are you ok?"

"Why do you scream so much? Does it really hurt that much?"

"Is your pain similar to a stomachache or headache?"

After listening to all these questions Hoja got angry and yelled, "Have any of you fallen from the roof?"

They all replied, "No."

Then Hoja said, "None of you can understand my condition unless you have fallen from a roof. Bring me someone who has fallen from a roof because only he can understand me."

Price of the King

The King and Hoja went to a Turkish bath and while they were washing they started chatting. As a tradition in Turkish baths, they were wearing their towels around their bellies.

The King asked, "Hoja tell me honestly, as if I were a fellow citizen, what do you think my price would be?"

Hoja smiled cunningly, "You are worth 10 coins."

Hearing this, the king reacted, "Oh, Hoja, that is not fair! This towel around my belly is worth 10 coins, how can my worth be 10 coins?"

Hoja laughed heartily, "Yes that is the price of the towel."

Hoja as Sales Man

Hoja decided to sell pickles. He thought to himself, "I'll load my donkey with the pickles and as I walk through the streets I will sell my pickles. The best part is the announcement. As I walk I will cheer merrily and make my announcement."

With all these thoughts he walked to town. When he was about to announce that he was selling pickles, the donkey started braying. The sound of the animal echoed all around. Whenever Hoja tried to make his announcement the donkey started braying.

Finally, his patience exhausted, Hoja spoke to his donkey, "I really wonder; are you the one who is going to sell the pickles or me?"

Dark at Night

One night Hoja stayed in his neighbor's house as a guest. As a tradition in Anatolia they laid their beds side by side on the floor to sleep all together in the living room. After the householder went to his bed then he asked Hoja to blow out the candle standing nearby. About to fall asleep, Hoja did not want to move so he ignored him and said, "You are a strange man. In this pitch darkness how can I find the candle?"

Hoja's Donkey Got Lost

One day Hoja's donkey got lost. What can poor Hoja do? He started wandering around. While he was looking for his donkey he started singing merrily.

Seeing him like this his neighbors asked in bewilderment, "Oh Hoja! What are you doing? How come a man sings merrily when his donkey is lost? Indeed you must have been crying desperately."

Giving a thought to their words Hoja replied, "My last hope is to find my donkey behind that mountain. There is no other place I have not looked. If I also cannot find it there, then you'll see how I will cry out."

Sound of the Coat

Early one morning when Hoja was leaving his house, one of his neighbors came to his walk-way. He asked, "Dear Hoja! There seems to be something wrong with you. Are you sick? What happened?"

Hoja replied, "No, I am not sick," and he tried to get rid of him.

However the curious neighbor insisted. Then Hoja said, "I have no problem. I would tell you if I had something wrong."

The neighbor kept on insisting, "But Hoja, last night I heard some noises coming from your house. Why was that? What was it?"

Hoja answered, "We had a fight, my wife and I."

The man nodded, "Those things are normal in relationships."

Hoja continued in a humble manner, "She was mad for no reason. Because I kept my silence she went crazy."

The neighbor asked curiously, "Then what happened?"

Hoja replied, "Nothing further happened. She was mad, that's all."

The neighbor insisted, "How about the noise?"

Hoja replied, "She went so crazy that she kicked my coat and the poor coat fell down the stairs. You probably must have heard that sound."

The neighbor replied in amusement, "Oh, Hoja! How can a coat make such a loud noise?"

Hoja smiled, "It was certainly the coat that fell down the stairs but I was in the coat."

Cabbage Soup

One day a stranger knocked at Hoja's door. Having no place to stay Hoja accepted him as a guest and gave him a place to stay. In response to Hoja's generosity the guest gave him a cabbage as a gift. From the big leaves of the cabbage Hoja made a very nice dish. They dined and chatted together and enjoyed each other's company. The next day the guest left.

The day after that another stranger arrived. He said "I'm the neighbor of the one who gave you the cabbage."

Hoja then invited the man for dinner and he made soup from the inner layers of the cabbage. After having the soup and staying in Hoja's house that night, the man left.

On the following day another visitor arrived who claimed to be the relative of the man who brought the cabbage. He stayed in Hoja's house and they ate whatever was left over from the cabbage. The next day he left.

In the following days, the visitors kept coming and going frequently. However Hoja's tolerance was exhausted and he got fed up with this cabbage story. He spoke to himself, "I understood that it is generous to give a cabbage but that is too much visiting and it is being overdone."

Finally 5 people visited Hoja claiming that they were the neighbor of the neighbor of the one who gave the cabbage. Hoja smiled and invited them into his house. He said "You are most welcome."

At night he prepared the dining table and brought a big stewpot full of plain water from the well. Hoja served the water in each bowl. None could understand what was going on.

One of them asked, "Oh Hoja what is this?" Hoja replied, "This is the water of the water of the cabbage."

Maybe Me!

One day, when Hoja was walking around in the market, he started chatting with a random guy. He enjoyed his company. He thought to himself, "How nice and positive he speaks! He made me forget my sorrow and pain."

When the time came to say good-bye Hoja asked, "Please forgive me but what is your name?"

The man got furious! "If you did not know me why did you approach and talk to me?"

Hoja was greatly surprised when he heard such an angry question. Hoja was a smart man, however, and full of clever answers. He quickly replied, "I saw your turban and it was the same as mine. Then I noticed your clothes; they were also the same as mine. Then I thought to myself, 'That man is maybe me.' That's why I approached and talked to you."

The Donkey

The mayor's donkey was lost. His men spread around to look for the animal. They also requested help from Hoja and sent him to the forest.

"Ok, let's look for it," he said, and settled into the search. While he was searching for the donkey, he was also singing.

When the people of the town saw him walking and singing in the forest they got curious and asked, "Oh Hoja, what are you doing?"

He answered comfortably that he was looking for a donkey. He couldn't convince anyone of this however. They asked "Oh Hoja! How is it possible to search for the donkey while you are singing?"

Hoja was an honest, fair man and he always spoke the truth. "Why are you so bewildered? The donkey is not mine but belongs to the mayor. If the donkey is not yours, then you sing while you look for it."

Why Does It Concern Me?

A man approached Hoja and said, "I saw a man carrying a tray full of desserts."

Hoja snubbed him, "Why does it concern me?"

The man did not understand what Hoja meant. "But Hoja he was taking it to your house."

Hoja snubbed him again, "So why does it concern you?"

Extending Tongs

One day, when Hoja was walking, he saw a man selling a sword for 20 gold coins. He asked why it was so expensive. "20 gold coins! Unbelievable! Why does it cost that much for a sword?"

The salesman replied in confidence, "It is a special sword. When you pull, it stretches 1 meter."

Hoja did not understand yet he did not react. The next day he came to the market place with a pair of old worn out tongs. He announced that he was selling them for 25 gold coins. Nobody paid attention. Hoja got angry and spoke, "Why are you so numb about the idea that I am selling these tongs for 25 gold coins? Only yesterday you were selling a sword for 20 gold coins."

They all reacted to his remark, saying, "Oh Hoja it had a specialty! When you pulled the sword, it lengthened 1 meter!"

Hoja smiled. "You don't know the specialty of this pair of tongs yet. It is also very special. You have no idea. Sometimes my scolding wife gets so out of control that she throws this pair of tongs towards me. Then it stretches up to 20 meters."

Smell of a Dream

One day Hoja was sitting at home and dreaming of soup. He spoke to himself, saying, "I wish there was soup now. I would add a mixture of pepper and oil but make it rich in mint and lemon. I would drink it merrily, spoon by spoon."

While he was dreaming, there was suddenly a knock at the door. He awoke, ran to the door and opened it. There stood the son of his neighbor carrying a bowl. When he saw the bowl, Hoja thought that it might be full of soup and got very happy. Looking to the bowl he asked, "Oh son! Have you brought me anything?"

The boy answered, "My mother is very sick. If you have any soup can you please give us some?"

After hearing the boy's request, Hoja was bewildered. "Oh my God! My neighbors are strange. They can even smell the soup in a dream."

I'm a Stranger in Here

On a business trip, Hoja visited a city far away. In this city he was a mere stranger. While he was running around trying to get things done, a man interrupted him. He stood in front of him and did not move. They were both perfect strangers to each other. Hoja thought that the stranger was going to say something important. Indeed he was in a hurry but he waited patiently for the man to speak.

The man spoke finally but he asked something irrelevant. He asked, "What is the day today?"

Upon hearing the man's question, Hoja got angry but he could not hurt his feelings or speak bitter words. He was in a hurry so he said, "I am a stranger to this town." After saying that, he walked away. The man looked at Hoja's back in bewilderment.

The Ox

An ox entered Hoja's field and ruined it. Taking his stick, Hoja ran after it but was not able to catch and hit it. Thus he felt upset. Talking to himself he murmured, "It doesn't matter. I'll eventually catch you."

After a couple of days he went to the market place and noticed a carriage pulled by an ox. He recognized that this was the ox which had ruined his field. He lifted his stick to beat the beast. Watching him do this, the owner ran towards Hoja in panic. "Oh Hoja what are you doing?"

Hoja snubbed the man and said, "Don't interfere; it knows what it has done!"

Bring My Coat

Hoja decided to go to the market place and took his donkey with him. On the way he needed to go to the toilet. Since there was no house or public toilet around, he had to go behind the bushes. To protect his coat, he took it off and laid it on the saddle. Before he walked away he told his donkey to take care of his coat.

Meanwhile a thief was walking by and saw Hoja leaving his coat unattended. The moment Hoja walked away he approached the donkey, and after stealing the coat, ran away.

When Hoja came out of the bushes he saw that his coat was missing. There was not even a trace of it. He was stunned and he got angry. It was very cold weather so in his frustration he took the saddle off the donkey and put it on himself to keep warm.

He said to his donkey, "Bring my coat and get your saddle back."

I Would Like to Die As Well

One day a neighbor invited Hoja to his house to drink some punch together. They sat together around the bowl. He gave a small spoon to Hoja and he took a ladle. Then they started drinking.

The neighbor's ladle filled and emptied one after the other while Hoja was struggling with a small spoon. He only drank air instead of the punch. On the other side, his neighbor was so pleased with the punch that he continuously said, "Oh! How delicious it is! I'm going to die of pleasure."

After watching him like this for a while, Hoja felt offended and his tolerance was finally exhausted. "Dear neighbor, please help me know what it is like. Now you take this small spoon and give that ladle to me so that I may also die of pleasure."

Hoja Goes Shopping

Hoja found a turban in the market place that he liked and intended to buy. Approaching the salesman, he asked the price. The salesman answered "10 coins."

Hoja told him to pack it. The moment he took the package he changed his mind because he saw a coat that he also liked. He asked the price of the coat. The salesman answered "It is also 10 coins."

Hoja said, "That is also very nice. Take this turban and give that coat to me." Then he took the coat and walked away.

As the salesman watched him walking away, he called out behind him, "Oh Hoja, where are you going without paying?"

Hoja answered, "Why have I given you the turban instead?"

The salesman answered in bewilderment, "But you did not pay for the turban either."

Hoja then got angry, saying, "I did not buy the turban. Why should I pay for something that I did not buy?"

Something Valuable

In the middle of the night, while Hoja and his wife were about to sleep, the wife heard some voices coming from the living room. She notified Hoja saying, "I think there is a thief in the house again. Do you hear him walking or have you already fallen asleep? Hey, don't you hear me?"

Hoja ignored her. It was never possible to guess Hoja's mood. His reaction changed from day to day. Some days Hoja was worried and cried out and some days he ignored the situation completely and slept through it. This was one of the days that he ignored whatever happened around him.

He kept calm and yawned slowly. Then he pulled the quilt over his head and turned to the other side of the bed. He spoke in confidence, "Why are you worried? Let's wait and see if he finds something valuable in the house. Then we can cry out and grab it from him."

Job Description

One day Hoja was sitting in a café in the town. A man ran towards him. He was anxious and excited. "Oh Hoja! You must come quickly! Your house is on fire!"

In those times there was no house insurance or established firehouse. Fire was a great danger. In such circumstances, when a person got this news, he should run back to his house and try to save it. However Hoja did not act upon this news.

Noticing Hoja's indifference, the people around him interfered. "Oh Hoja, your house is on fire but you still sit here. Aren't you going to do anything?"

He yawned and spoke, "Don't get me into trouble with my wife. She made our job descriptions clear. I'm responsible for the things outside the house while she is responsible for the things inside the house. I have not gone mad enough to mess with her business."

The Cure for Insomnia

Hoja's wife was complaining because their child was not sleeping. She asked Hoja for help and insisted that he find a solution. She was upset and frustrated.

After listening to his wife, Hoja gave her a book to read. His wife looked at the book and then spoke in disappointment, "Please have some mercy. I'm deeply troubled but you're mocking me."

Hoja said, "I'm trying to help you. Just listen to what I say and follow my instructions. Read this book to the child and he will fall asleep. Women are strange creatures. They ask for a solution but do not like it when it is offered."

After hearing his words, his wife stopped objecting. "Ok, I will listen to you. Give me the book and I'll read it to the kid."

Unexpectedly the book cured the child's sleeping issue. He suddenly started sleeping. Upon seeing this she asked, "He slept! How is that possible?"

Hoja answered, "Don't ask too much about it. I know the trick of the book because of my experiences. I sometimes read it to the audience in the mosque and everybody starts sleeping."

The Feed of the Donkey

One day Hoja and his wife had a fight. He said to his wife that she should feed the donkey. However the woman did not like the idea and they started a fight. Both insisted that the other should feed the donkey.

Hoja said, "You should feed the animal."

The wife insisted, "No, today is your turn and you should feed the donkey."

Then they made a bet. Whoever spoke first should feed the donkey. To be able to keep herself from speaking and win the bet, she went for a visit to the neighbor's.

After she left the house, thieves broke in and started collecting whatever they saw. Hoja did not say a word so as to not lose the bet. He simply watched the thieves and did not interfere.

After they had collected whatever they found the thieves left the house merrily. When the sun was setting, his wife came back to the house. Finding the house empty, she started crying out after her stolen possessions. As she spoke, Hoja said, "Since you spoke first then you've lost the bet. Now go and feed the donkey."

King's Dream

In times long ago, whoever the king saw in his dream he used to behead. Hearing about this terrible habit of the king's, Hoja decided to leave town.

His neighbors, however, objected to his leaving. They said, "Please Hoja, don't go! You are the only one the king listens to and obeys."

It was indeed true that Hoja was the only one who could keep the king under control. Hoja did not want to risk his life, however, and he picked up his bag to leave. Before he left he said, "Find someone else to take my place and count on him instead of me. I can deal with the king in the morning but is it in my hands not to appear in his dream?"

King's Elephant

The king brought an elephant to the town. However the elephant turned out to be a real problem. It did not let anyone rest or sleep because it never stopped eating. People got fed up with the beast and they wanted to stop looking after it. They gathered together and tried to find a solution. One of them said, "Let's ask Hoja to talk to the king about the elephant." They all agreed and visited Hoja.

After listening to them, Hoja also liked the idea and wanted to help them. A group gathered together to escort Hoja and they all started walking towards the palace. As they approached the palace, however, people started slipping away one by one. The moment they reached the door, Hoja turned to look behind and saw that there was no one left following him. Hoja got angry.

When Hoja was accepted in the king's chamber, he was asked the purpose of his visit. Hoja replied, "I came here to thank you. We are so happy with your gift, the elephant. However the elephant is not happy about being alone. He requires a partner."

Upon hearing this, the king interrupted suddenly. "Do you want a female partner for the elephant?" he asked in an excited tone. Then he happily announced, "So be it! That is easy."

After this conversation, Hoja left the king's court and headed towards the town. When they saw him coming, all his neighbors surrounded him and started asking questions: "Have you told our wish to the king? Will we be able to get rid of the elephant and give it back finally?"

Ignoring their question, Hoja kept on walking towards his house and said, "Calm down. Why are you all so anxious? I have good news for you. A female elephant will be joining him soon."

The Cat and the Axe

For several mornings Hoja brought nice ingredients to the house for his wife to cook for him. However, whenever he came back home in the evenings, his wife only served plain soup and bread. Poor Hoja could not have a nice dinner in his house. He could not talk about this problem to anyone. Whenever he asked what had happened to the groceries he brought she answered that the cat ate the food.

One day he again heard the same answer and grabbed the axe in panic, hiding it in the wardrobe. Watching this, his wife asked curiously, "Oh Hoja! What are you doing?"

He answered firmly, "If the cat continuously steals the food which costs only 3 coins then it will definitely steal an axe worth 40 coins."

Beaten by a Stick

A soldier was caught while he was drinking alcohol. He was brought to the palace in front of the king. Hoja was also present there.

As his guilt was announced the king started yelling and swearing at the soldier. "Did you think that we would never catch you and you could get away with this? Now I will give you a lesson that you'll never forget." Then turning to the other soldiers he commanded, "Lay him down and hit his bare feet 1000 times with a stick. "

When he heard this, Hoja started chuckling. As much as he tried to hide his smile or stop laughing, he could not help himself. This did not escape the king's notice. Turning to Hoja with an angry face he started yelling at him, "Do you criticize my decision?"

Hoja smiled and said, "As you do not laugh at such a decision it means that you either have never been beaten by a stick or you don't know how to count."

Nothing

When Hoja was working as a judge at the court, two men came to see him, complaining about each other.

The first man said, "Dear Hoja, I was walking by and this man was carrying a wood basket to his house. However the wood basket was heavy and he was struggling to grab and place it on his back. Seeing him struggling, I wanted to help him so I asked him what would he give me if I helped him place it on his back. He said, "Nothing." After hearing his answer, I agreed to hold his basket and place it on his back. Then I asked for my payment. He shrugged and ignored me." Then he turned to Hoja and said, "Now I ask you, shouldn't I ask for my share and my payment?"

After listening to this, Hoja interrupted. "Yes you are right. You'll get what you have asked for but before I give my decision, please take hold of the edge of the carpet and lift it. Then tell me what you see."

Upon Hoja's instructions, the man lifted the carpet's edge and answered, "Nothing."

Then Hoja said, "Now you take it and leave the court. Is there anything still due from the payment?"

To Be Saved from Death

One day Hoja came home in the dark of night and saw a shadow in the garden. He thought that it might be a thief again. He yelled at his wife, "Oh wife! Bring my bow and arrows! I saw a thief in the garden."

When his wife heard him, she brought his bow and arrows and he shot towards the shadow in the garden. After the shadow was hit by the arrow it fell down. Hoja was relieved that he had successfully wiped out the danger by killing the thief. Since it was dark, he did not dare go near the shadow.

The next morning he went to the garden and looked where he thought he had hit the thief. Surprisingly he saw that it was his coat which his wife had washed yesterday. Meanwhile his wife was standing at the door of the house waiting for the news. He turned to his wife and said, "This is a day to celebrate. I'm saved from death. I hit my own coat. Luckily I was not in it."

Lost

Neighbors came to visit Hoja. They decided to make fun of him. Their real intention was to see his reaction. They said, "We noticed that your wife has lost her mind."

Hoja started thinking about what he had just heard. When his silence had lasted a long time, one of them asked, "Hoja, what are you thinking?"

Hoja smiled and said, "This information of yours arouses my curiosity. I cannot stop wondering what my wife really lost, when she had no mind to lose."

Thieves and the Donkey

One day Hoja was walking to the market with his donkey. He was singing merrily. He was enjoying singing so much that he forgot himself and the donkey. Two thieves, seeing him walking alone, snuck up on him from behind. They untied the rope from the donkey and tied it on one of the thief's neck. For some time he walked as if he was the donkey while the other got away with the animal.

After a while Hoja turned back and saw the thief instead of his donkey. Hoja asked in surprise, "How is that possible? Who are you?"

The thief responded: "Oh Hoja once I was a human but I told a lie and I turned into a donkey. Today was the last day of my punishment. Now it is over and I am turned back into a human again. Please set me free."

Since a human was no use to him, Hoja liked the idea and accepted his offer immediately. He thought to himself, "There must be something good in it." So he came back his house holding only the rope left from his donkey.

After a couple of days Hoja went to the market. While he was walking around he came across his donkey. It had been put on sale by a merchant. First he felt surprised then he came back to his senses and approached the donkey. He spoke into its ear, "Dear brother, it seems that being a donkey is your destiny. Tell me what you have done now?"

Go Further

Hoja was fed up with his wife's nagging. One night after they went to bed she said, "Hoja, can you go further?"

After hearing what she said, Hoja thought this must be a blessing from God. Thus he suddenly got up, took a few of his belongings and set out on the road. Neither the house nor his wife was his concern any more. He walked away without looking back.

After 2 hours he came across one of his neighbors and remembered his house. He stopped him and said, "Now you are heading towards our town. When you arrive, go to my house and ask my wife to send a message telling me if she wants me to come back home. Otherwise I'll go further."

What Is There to Be Afraid of?

While Hoja and his wife were sleeping they heard thieves speaking. One of them said, "Now we'll go directly into the stable. First we'll slaughter Hoja's cow and then we'll go into the house and kill Hoja. After that we'll rob the house. Have you all brought your knives with you? Are you ready to attack?"

They answered, "Yes!"

Hoja felt horrified when he heard this. His heart raced. The situation seemed terrible and his life was in danger. He coughed loudly. Hearing his cough, the thieves realized that Hoja was awake and aware of their plan so they ran away.

Seeing his reaction, his wife said, "Oh, Hoja, why are you scared?"

Hoja got angry and replied, "Look at you, asking me what there is to be scared of! Ask me and the cow!"

The Candle Light

The delivery pains of Hoja's wife started late at night. Neighbors and the midwife were called. All started working together to help the delivery. Since there was no electricity in those times, they had to light the room with a candle. Thus they gave the candle to Hoja to hold and light the room.

After the baby was born the midwife announced that another baby was coming. Immediately, Hoja blew the candle out and the room was suddenly pitch-dark.

Since they could see nothing and could not help with the delivery, the women got angry and asked, "Have you lost your mind? Why did you blow out the candle? Now everything will be messed up. How can we help her deliver the other baby?"

In response Hoja said, "Whoever sees the light is coming. Is this place a hostel for the homeless?"

Visits a Lot

One day Hoja's neighbors came for a visit. They said, "Hoja, we hear and see that your wife is visiting many houses. She is either in one house or in another. People are gossiping about her."

When Hoja heard this he smiled cunningly. "I don't think that this can be true. If she were visiting that many houses, she would definitely come and visit our house."

Angel of Death

One day Hoja fell sick. He realized that he would die soon. He was scared. He called his wife and said, "Oh dear wife, my life has come to an end. Now please go and wear your finest clothes and put some make up on your face. Then come and sit beside me."

His wife responded in astonishment, "How is that possible? When you are about to die and meet the Angle of Death how can I merrily put make up on my face and wear my finest clothes?"

Hoja smiled and said, "Please listen to me. If you don't do it I won't speak to you again. It is certain that the Angel of Death will come to take me but it is also possible that he may like you and take you with him."

If She Was Not Dead

Hoja's wife went to another town to visit her relatives. After some time, news arrived that his wife was dead. The neighbors heard the news and felt sad. Since it was not good news they started thinking about how to inform Hoja.

They went to visit him. In a quiet, polite manner they told him that his wife was dead. They expected him to cry and feel sad.

However Hoja did not react. Instead he said, "We are old people and eventually either she or I was going to die. If she were not dead, she would be attending my funeral."

Spring

A man said to Hoja, "Oh Hoja these people are strange, even disgraceful. Some of them complain about the cold in winter, some of them complain about the heat in summer."

Hoja got angry when he heard this and said, "Silence man! No one complains about the spring."

Thief and the Prayer

One night when Hoja was about to sleep he heard a thief walking on the roof. He made his wife wake up and said, "Last night when I came home you were in a deep sleep. You did not hear me although I knocked at the door for some time. When I realized that I wouldn't be able to wake you up, I said a special prayer and by holding up the moonlight, I sneaked into the house.

His wife asked "Which prayer helped you to hold up the moonlight like a rope?" So Hoja told her.

Meanwhile the thief was listening to them. He quickly memorized the prayer and repeated it to himself. Then, while trying to hold up the moonlight he attempted to break into the house. Since holding up the moonlight was impossible he fell off the roof.

Hearing the terrible sound, Hoja ran to the garden and yelled to his wife, "Bring the candle I caught the thief!"

Lying on the ground like a wreck the thief raised his head and spoke, "Oh Hoja, you need not hurry to catch me! As long as you have such a prayer and I have such a mind, I cannot stand up or run away from here."

Weak Old Horse

One day the king decided to go on a hunting trip and take Hoja with him. The king and his men had fast and firm horses but they gave a weak old horse to Hoja. While they ran and flew away, Hoja had to follow them behind slowly.

Suddenly it started to rain. It was pouring heavily. The men with their fast horses disappeared quickly. However it was no use to kick or beat the poor old horse. It would be going nowhere. Realizing this, Hoja took off all his clothes to protect them from getting wet and put them in the saddlebag. Since he was naked, he hid himself behind the bush and waited for the rain to stop. It was a summer rain so it stopped after a short while and the sun shone again.

After the sun came out, Hoja confidently put his dry clothes back on. Coming out of the hostel where they had taken refuge, the king and his men appeared in a short while as well. They were bewildered to see that Hoja's clothes were completely dry and he was calmly waiting for them. The king was so mortified that he could not help asking how that was possible.

Hoja replied, "Never be deceived by the appearance. There are a lot of weak old horses which turn out to be thunderbolts when the time comes." They all believed what they heard him say and made the weak old creature the lead horse to walk ahead of the other horses.

One day the king decided to go out hunting so he took the weak old horse with him. It did not matter how hard he tried, he could not make the horse run but he was somehow able to arrive at the hunting area.

Suddenly the dark clouds appeared and a storm broke out. The old horse did not care at all. Instead of running fast as Hoja had described, it walked backwards. The king became wet because of the heavy rain. He got frustrated and angry and decided to make Hoja pay for it.

He came back without hunting anything. He immediately summoned Hoja to teach him a lesson and punish him because of lying to the king. As soon as the king saw Hoja, he started shouting and swearing.

Hoja also decided to teach the king a lesson so he said, "Dear king! I'm sorry to say it but this was your mistake. You should have acted according to the situation. Noticing the horse does not turn into a thunderbolt, you should have turned yourself into Hoja, and hidden behind the bushes after taking off all your clothes and placing them in your saddlebag."

Bow Down in Front of the Lord

One day Hoja decided to travel. He planned to stay in a hostel on his way. However the hostel was an old ruin which seemed likely to collapse at any time. Fear overtook him as he entered. He tried to hide it but he could not convince and comfort himself.

He felt so unsafe that finally he asked the hostel owner, "Your roof is making a lot of squeaky sounds like a baby's crib that is swinging from one side to the other."

The hostel owner ignored Hoja and said mockingly, "Do not speak like that. You have misinterpreted the situation. The squeaky sound you hear is not a crib. The roof is just praying to the Lord."

Hoja said mockingly, as he looked at the roof, was this: "What would happen to us if this roof gets so much absorbed in its prayers so as to go ecstatic with love and bow down in front of the Lord?"

The Donkey Can Read

A man gave a donkey as a gift to the king. Some people who wanted to humiliate Hoja decided to use this as an opportunity. They told the king that a talented and special donkey like this can even learn to read if a scholar such as Hoja trains it. The king liked the idea and did not want to waste the opportunity of mocking and humiliating Hoja. Thus he summoned him and gave the donkey to him to be trained.

The king said "From now on you have the responsibility. Teach it how to read and turn it into a literate donkey."

Taking the donkey by his side, Hoja calmly walked back his house. For some time he searched for a way out of this puzzle. Then he found a solution. He made a big book with leather pages and he let the donkey starve for a few days. Then he placed some barley grains in between the pages and fed the animal by turning the pages. After sometime the animal got used to this feeding style so it started turning pages with his mouth, one by one, eating the barley grains and braying in anticipation of getting more when it arrived at the last page.

The day before the examination, Hoja let the donkey go hungry for the night. The next day he took the donkey with him to the palace. As he arrived at the palace, he put the leather book on the table. The donkey started turning the pages and braying because it could not find any grains to eat in between the pages. When it turned the last page it started braying loudly.

After the donkey's exhibition, Hoja said, "As you can see, the donkey read the book as he turned the pages."

All of them were bewildered. Some envious people asked, however, "Yes we saw that it was reading but we did not understand a word what it was reading."

Hoja then smiled and said, "Of course you don't understand what it reads. Since it is a donkey, it read the book according to its own language. To understand what it said you should also be a donkey."

Blessing of God

One day Hoja was sitting in front of his window watching the people passing by. Suddenly a heavy rain began to pour down. People started running away and trying to find shelter from the storm. Meanwhile, Hoja noticed one of his neighbors was hurrying to his house to avoid getting wet. Hoja immediately opened his window and yelled at him, "You call yourself a literate man but you don't know that the rain is the blessing of God. Is it wise to run away from the blessing of God?"

After hearing Hoja's words, the poor fellow had to stop. He thought that Hoja was right. Besides, he did not want to give an opportunity to Hoja to mock him afterwards so he slowed down and walked slowly to his house instead of running. Thus he got soaking wet all the way down to his underwear.

What comes around goes around! After a couple of days, another rain storm broke out and Hoja was caught on the way back to his home. This time his neighbor was inside his house and he was watching outside. Seeing Hoja hurrying to his home to avoid getting wet, he opened his window and yelled at him, "Oh Hoja I see that you are running so fast that your feet barely touch the ground. Why do you run away from the blessing of God?"

Hoja replied confidently, "My dear friend, don't misinterpret the situation. Who is running away from the blessing of God? I am trying not to step on God's blessing; that's why I am hurrying and keeping my feet off the ground."

Which One is My Foot?

The children of the town went to the lake and put their feet into the water. They started joking, "So you see! We have all lost our feet. Where are our feet? How are we going to find our feet?"

First they were having fun and then they started fighting. They were fighting over their feet. "Where is my foot? No this is your foot. How am I going to find my foot?"

Hoja was passing by and heard their fight. He grabbed a wooden stick and put it into the water and started hitting each foot he saw. All the children screamed in pain and pulled their feet out of the water. He kept hitting feet with his stick until the last kid took his feet out of the water.

Then turning to the kids he said, "So did you see how quickly you found your feet? Now the fight is over."

The Quilt

One night Hoja suddenly woke up to terrible sounds coming from outside. His wife was awakened as well. They both hurried to the window and saw that a group of men were fighting. It was cold and rainy.

He told his wife, "They will harm each other. Let me go out, give some advice and try to solve the conflict."

His wife objected and tried to stop him. "Don't go out. It may be harmful, especially so late at night. Go back to bed."

Ignoring her, Hoja walked out. He went in between the fighting gang and asked about what was going on. They were fighting about a quilt. It was cold and there was only one quilt so everyone was claiming that it belonged to him.

Nobody listened to Hoja's advice to find peace so Hoja took the quilt and silently walked back to his house. Nobody noticed that he walked away. After Hoja came into the house his wife told him that the fight was suddenly over. Hoja smiled after hearing the news and said, "As you see, the quilt is gone so the fight is gone."

The Yogurt and the Vinegar

One day Hoja set out on the way with a man. They bought a bowl of yogurt together. After some time they decided to rest and eat the yogurt. The man took some sugar out of his bag.

He said "I will only add sugar to my side not to the whole."

Upon hearing this, Hoja spoke in bewilderment, "How is that possible? If you put sugar on some you will put sugar all over the yogurt!"

However the man did not want to listen or understand Hoja and completely ignored him. Realizing this, Hoja said, "Then I will add vinegar to my side."

In a panic, the man interfered and said, "Oh Hoja! What are you talking about? How can you add vinegar to the yogurt but only to your side?"

Getting angry Hoja said, "Then don't speak this "your half" nonsense and add sugar all over the yogurt."

The Blind Fight

When Hoja was young he liked making jokes. Once he saw 3 blind men sitting alongside the street. He approached them holding a small bag of coins. He shook the bag in front of them and said, "Take this bag of coins and share it among you," but he did not actually give the bag to any of them.

Naturally they thought that the bag had been given to one of them so they asked each other who got the bag. "Who has the bag? I don't have it. Did you get the bag?"

Then they started blaming each other for lying about the bag. One man shouted at the other two, "The bag is taken by one of you or both of you. You are definitely lying."

With their greediness for money, they kept up a terrible fight, hitting each other, screaming and swearing. They lost their self-control.

Watching them Hoja said, "That must be what they call a blind fight."

The Taste of the Grape

One day Hoja visited the vineyard and left after loading two bags full of grapes on his donkey. As he approached his house, the kids of the town surrounded him and wanted to have some grapes. He gave some grapes to the kids but they were not satisfied and asked for more.

He compared the amount of grapes he now had with the number of kids and realized that the grapes would run out if he gave more so he said, "It does not matter whether there are more grapes or less; all grapes taste the same."

Share by God or by Hoja

The children of the town bought a bag of walnuts but they could not share them. Thus they started a fight. Meanwhile Hoja was passing by. When the children saw him they surrounded him and asked for help. "Hoja, we cannot share the walnuts. Please share them out."

When he heard their request, Hoja asked, "Do you want me to share the walnuts in my way or in God's way?"

The children answered, "Share in God's way." Then Hoja dug his hand into the bag and took out a few walnuts and threw them to the children. Some children received two some got one and some took no walnuts.

This was how Hoja finished sharing the walnuts. However the children were not satisfied with this way of sharing. They opposed him and said, "Oh Hoja, this is unfair. We do not accept this."

Hoja smiled and said, "It is your fault! You have chosen the 'share by God' way. This is how God shares things. He gives as much as he likes and we can never know who should get more, less or none. Now you either accept your share by God or accept the share by me."

Take My Hand

One day Hoja went to a picnic with his friends. Suddenly they heard a man yelling and asking for help. They ran towards the sound and saw someone familiar, the stingiest man in their town, had fallen into the water by accident. He was struggling to get out of the water. Since he did not know how to swim he was about to drown.

The people tried to help him and shouted, "Give us your hand, give us your hand." Strangely the man did not give his hand and kept on struggling.

Luckily, Hoja arrived in time and he pushed the crowd aside. He approached the man and said, "Take my hand, take my hand!" Suddenly he grabbed Hoja's hand. He was out of the water and safe.

After the hustle was over, the people gathered around Hoja and asked how he managed to save him. Hoja said, "You don't know how stingy he is. He only takes but never gives."

The Punishment of the Fox

Hoja needed money so he decided to work as imam during the month of Ramadan. He visited several villages but no village wanted him. Finally he arrived tired and exhausted at a village. He was starving and had no more energy to move.

Suddenly he noticed an angry crowd screaming and shouting. As he approached he saw that they had caught a fox. They were so fed up with it and were trying to find a way to punish it. Then they noticed Hoja and decided to ask him for a proper punishment. Hoja gladly accepted and said, "Oh don't kill it. I have a much better punishment for it." Then he grabbed the fox, put his own turban on its head and covered it with his coat. Then he let it go. The fox ran away and disappeared immediately.

Now the people were shocked. They asked furiously, "Oh Hoja, what have you done?"

He replied smilingly, "I have punished him so terribly that you cannot even imagine. I made him wear my garments. Now you can be sure that he will be recognized and kicked out of every village he visits so he will starve to death like me."

Grape

One day Hoja had a visitor. He prepared a nice dinner for him. They chatted together. Long story short, they had a nice time together. When they were about to sleep, the man wanted to eat some grapes but he could not say it directly so he started a song. "In our town people eat grapes. They eat grapes before they sleep. La La La La"

Hoja was tired and he did not want to serve grapes at this time of night. He also answered with a song in the same tune. "We do not have such a habit. We hide the grapes and eat them in the morning. La La La"

I Know What To Do!

The town was fed up with the king and his cruelty. They were trying to think of a way out but they were desperate. Finally one morning Hoja went to see the king. As he met the king he directly said, "Look at me and tell me! Are you going to leave this town or not?"

The King replied in bewilderment and frustration, "I am not leaving; what are you going to do?"

Hoja replied, "If you don't leave I know what I will do."

The king got angrier and asked further, "Tell me what you will do?"

Hoja replied, "Nothing! If you don't go, I will leave the town and take all the people along with me."

The Wife's Nagging

One night Hoja wanted to chat with his wife. He asked, "My dear wife, please tell me, what was our neighbor, the tailor, Mehmet's name?"

His wife replied in bewilderment, "Oh Hoja, you have just said his name, Mehmet."

"I am mistaken for a second. I was going to ask you his job." he said.

His wife was stunned. "You've gone weird again. Haven't you said that he was a tailor?"

Hoja said, "Sorry again. I was going to ask you where he was living."

Getting even more surprised his wife said, "You can easily make a person crazy. You've just said that he is our neighbor."

Finally Hoja said, "Oh, now I understand! That is what they call 'wife's nagging'. You continuously complain. I cannot even have a couple of words with you."

You Could Not Be Half of Your Son!

One day Hoja visited a city to handle his business related to government. He struggled hard to handle it but he could not finalize it.

One of his friends told him to attend the morning prayers for 40 days in the *big* mosque and on the 41st day his wish would definitely come true. Listening to his friend's advice, Hoja did as he was told. However his business was still not finalized. Days passed and he had to stay longer in the town.

On one of these days, he went into a *small* mosque to pray to soothe his anger. After he finished his prayer, he went out and immediately got the good news that his job was done.

After hearing this good news, he directly went to the *big* mosque. Standing in front of its gate he spoke, "Shame on you! You could not measure up to half of your son!"

Three Scholars

Three scholars came to visit the town. They met Hoja. They all dined and chatted together. They wanted to test Hoja, however, so one of them asked, "Tell us, where is the middle of the earth?"

Hoja took his stick and showed the point beneath the legs of his donkey. "There it is."

The scholar laughed in a mocking manner and said, "So how do you know that it is the middle of the earth?"

Staring in the scholar's eyes Hoja replied in confidence, "If you don't believe me then go and measure it." The first scholar had to shut up.

Then the second scholar asked, "Tell us how many stars are there up in the sky?"

Showing his donkey Hoja said, "There is the same amount of stars up in the sky as the number of hairs on my donkey."

The scholar opposed that answer and said, "Nonsense! How can you prove this?"

Ignoring him, Hoja said, "If you don't believe me, go on, count them. If you find one hair more or less I am here." The second scholar had to shut his mouth as well.

The third scholar asked, "Tell me, how much hair do I have in my beard?"

Hoja said, "That's so easy. The same amount of hair as my donkey has on the tip of its tail."

In bewilderment the third scholar reacted, "Now you have exaggerated! You can never prove this."

Hoja smiled and said, "No? Indeed it is so simple. We pluck one hair from your beard and one from my donkey and we keep going like that. Then we'll see if the amounts match or not. Then we'll see who is right."

With all of these answers, the scholars were surprised and stopped asking questions. Bowing their heads down, they left the town and never came back.

Hunting Water Buffalo with a Crow

One day Hoja saw two kids fighting over a crow that they had hunted. He felt pity on the small creature and bought it from the kids in exchange for a coin.

After that he released the crow. It flew and perched on the head of a water buffalo. Hoja smiled when he saw this and spoke to himself, "Well done, my beautiful trained bird. My black hawk hunted a water buffalo for me." After he said these words he took the water buffalo to his stable.

People saw him taking the animal to his stable and informed the man who had lost and was in search of his buffalo. The man was tired of looking for his buffalo so he happily arrived at Hoja's door. Hoja, however, did not want to give the animal back. He said, "Hunting is accepted as a good deed by our religion and my bird has hunted a buffalo. Thus the animal is mine. If you insist further, go to the court and sue me."

Consequently, the owner of the buffalo went to the court and sued Hoja. He told about the situation. Hoja knew that it was easy to bribe the judge so he sent a message to the judge and promised to give him a bowl of butter made of buffalo milk. After receiving such a promise, the judge gave his decision in favor of Hoja. As much as the owner cried and begged, he could not make the judge listen to him.

The next day Hoja sent the bowl of butter to the judge as he promised. The judge was so happy with the butter and started eating it day and night. However, as he reached the middle of the bowl, a smell of excrement filled the room. As he dug deeper in the bowl, he saw the other half of the bowl was full of excrement. Enraged and angry, he summoned Hoja. Showing the bowl he asked, "Oh Hoja what is this? "

Hoja replied "It is the excretion of a buffalo."

Now, the judge got even more frustrated. "What are you talking about? Don't you have any shame offering and making me eat buffalo excretion?"

Hoja replied in confidence, "You have not eaten it today but two days ago when you decided the case in my favor, by accepting that a water buffalo can be hunted by a crow."

After that, Hoja left the judge and took the buffalo back to its owner.

Between the Man and the God

Every morning Hoja used to pray to God. "Oh God, send me 100 gold coins. If you send 99 I won't accept it."

His neighbor was a rich merchant and he used to hear that prayer. One day he decided to play a trick. He decided to give Hoja 99 gold coins and see whether or not he rejected it. Thus he got up early in the morning, climbed up to Hoja's roof and threw 99 gold coins in Hoja's lap.

Then he started listening to Hoja counting the coins. Hoja talked to himself, "God sent these 99 coins so he will definitely send one more and finally it will be completed up to 100. I accept them as they have arrived."

Hearing this, the merchant panicked. He understood that he had lost the coins so he knocked at Hoja's door and asked for his gold coins back.

Hoja ignored him and said, "You swindler! Have you gone mad? What have you given to me and now you ask for it to be returned?"

The merchant got more anxious. He did not know what to do! He started begging. "Oh Hoja such an honest Muslim like you would never deny the coins he received."

Hoja said, "Sorry, I have not received gold coins from you and I don't know what you are talking about."

The merchant then said, "I will go to the court and sue you."

Hoja said, "Well, I would come with you but the court is far from here and I cannot go there on foot. Besides I don't have clean, new clothes to wear."

Thus the merchant bought him a donkey, new clothes and a fur coat so they could both go to the court.

The merchant confessed what he had done to test Hoja and how the story ended. He asked for his gold coins to be returned to him.

The judge asked Hoja for his story. Hoja said, "Sir, this man is my neighbor. I think he heard me when I was counting my gold coins in the morning. As it is obvious from my clothes and everyone knows, I don't need his money. Can you imagine such a man giving me such an amount of gold for nothing in return? Who would believe such a thing? I know his strange nature better than anyone. He claims that everything belongs to him. He can even claim that this fur coat I'm wearing belongs to him."

Upon hearing this, the merchant interrupted, "It is true! I bought it for him."

Hoja continued, "God knows! Now he will claim that even my donkey belongs to him."

The merchant started jumping up and down in anger. He said, "Dear Lord! Sir… It is true that I bought the donkey for him."

The judge got frustrated and angry with the claims of the merchant and had him removed from the court. In this way, the court was over in favor of Hoja.

Hoja got back to his house with the taste of victory. Then he called the merchant and gave his gold coins back to him. He said, "Never ever come in between the God and the man and don't hurt anyone."

As he was trying to test Hoja, the merchant was the one who was tested.

Sources

- Name of the Book: Nasreddin HocaHikâyeleri
  Editor: OrhanVeliKanık
  Publisher: YKY (YapıKrediYayınları)
  ISBN:978-975-08-0543-7
- Name of the Book: Nasreddin Hoca
  Editor: KemalÖzer
  Publisher: ArkadaşKitaplar
  ASIN: B002AU7EX4
- Name of the Book: Nasreddin Hodja
  Publisher: MertBasımYayıncılıkDagıtımveReklamcılık Tic. Ltd. Şti.
  Editor: Mehmet Güldiz
  ISBN: 975-285-188-6
- Name of the Book: Nasreddin HocaileFıkırFıkır
  Editor: Ali Faruk
  Publisher: ÇilekKitaplar- Hayat YayıncılıkIletişim, Yapım, EgitimHizmetlerive Tic. Ltd. Şti.ISBN: 978-605-118-048-9

Appendix

Footnotes

[1] Madrasa: is the Arabic word for any type of educational institution, whether secular or religious (of any religion).
[2] Imam: A male prayer leader in a mosque
[3] Hoja means scholar in Turkish. Hoja is his title not his name. At those times there were no surnames so people were known by their titles. In small letters the word "hoja" is used as adjective and in caps lock "Hoja" is used as his name.
[4] Because of this famous story a wall is standing in the grave of Nasreddin Hoja, greeting his visitors.
[5] Quince: a very hard apple-like fruit
[6] Timur: Tarmashirin Khan, Emir Timur (9 April 1336 – 18 February 1405), historically known as Tamerlane was a Turkish ruler, a powerful king. It is said that Nasreddin Hoja lived in his time so his name is used in the stories often. However this is not certain, so the word "king" is used instead of the name Timur.
[7] He is the friend of Prophet Moses. According to a known story, Khidr arrives on time to help whoever is in need and prays to God to make their wishes to come true.

Printed in Great Britain
by Amazon